For additional information and ordering, contact:

John D. Sanabria
Phone: (407) 552-7582
Email:
jsanabria747@hotmail.com

www.ingramcontent.com/pod-product-compliance
Lightning Source LLC
Chambersburg PA
CBHW021138260726
48656CB00023B/662
* 9 7 8 1 7 1 8 6 4 1 4 5 7 *